W2-3

ABDO
Publishing Company

CIRCULATORY
System

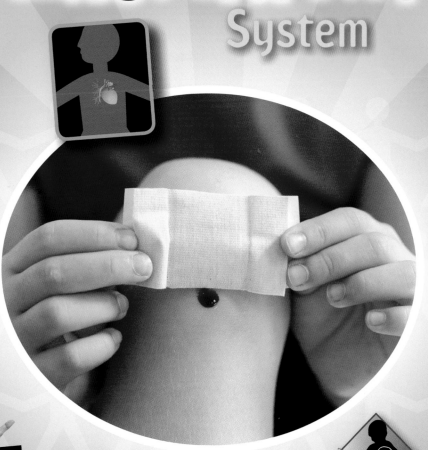

BODY SYSTEMS

Buddy BOOKS
Body Systems

A Buddy Book by Sarah Tieck

VISIT US AT
www.abdopublishing.com

Published by ABDO Publishing Company, 8000 West 78th Street, Edina, Minnesota 55439.

Printed in the United States of America, North Mankato, Minnesota.
092010
012011

 PRINTED ON RECYCLED PAPER

Coordinating Series Editor: Rochelle Baltzer
Contributing Editors: Megan M. Gunderson, BreAnn Rumsch, Marcia Zappa
Graphic Design: Jenny Christensen
Cover Photograph: *iStockphoto*: ©iStockphoto.com/timsa.
Interior Photographs/Illustrations: *Eighth Street Studio* (pp. 5, 22); *iStockphoto*:
    ©iStockphoto.com/damaianty (p. 11), ©iStockphoto.com/Eraxion (pp. 11, 15),
    ©iStockphoto.com/Fotosmurf03 (p. 30), ©iStockphoto.com/johnwoodcock (p. 7),
    ©iStockphoto.com/jsmith (p. 27), ©iStockphoto.com/lovleah (p. 27),
    ©iStockphoto.com/Lowryn (p. 13), ©iStockphoto.com/mammamaart (p. 25),
    ©iStockphoto.com/monkeybusinessimages (p. 30), ©iStockphoto.com/MrRoboto
    (p. 17), ©iStockphoto.com/nano (p. 22), ©iStockphoto.com/nicolesy (p. 9),
    ©iStockphoto.com/polygraphus (p. 23); *Shutterstock*: Blamb (p. 19), hkannn (p. 21),
    Gina Sanders (p. 29); *U.S. National Library of Medicine* (p. 23).

Library of Congress Cataloging-in-Publication Data

Tieck, Sarah, 1976-
 Circulatory system / Sarah Tieck.
   p. cm. -- (Body systems)
 ISBN 978-1-61613-497-6
 1. Cardiovascular system--Juvenile literature. I. Title.
 QP103.T54 2011
 612.1--dc22
                          2010019665

Table of Contents

Amazing Body...4

Teamwork 6

Giving Life 8

Protecting and Healing 12

From the Heart 14

A Long Journey... 18

Brain Food.. 22

Glug Glug 24

An Important System................................. 28

Healthy Body Files 30

Important Words....................................... 31

Web Sites... 31

Index... 32

Amazing Body

Your body is amazing! It does thousands of things each day. You can run, smile, and see because your body parts work together.

Groups of body parts make up body systems. Each system does important work. The circulatory system sends blood to every part of your body. Let's learn more about it!

Your circulatory system is located all over the inside of your body!

Teamwork

Your heart, blood, and blood vessels work together in your circulatory system. Your brain helps out, too! Without you even thinking about it, your brain helps control your heartbeat.

Each time your heart beats, it sends blood through your body. This **process** keeps you alive.

Your brain can survive about six minutes without fresh blood pumping in. After that, brain cells begin to die.

WORD OF MOUTH

YOUR CIRCULATORY SYSTEM

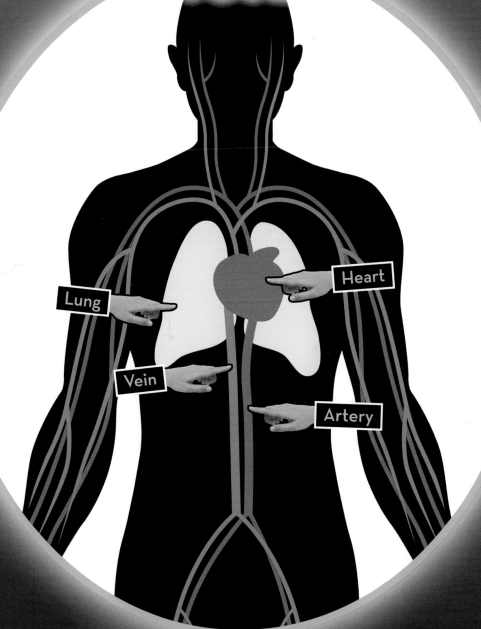

When you breathe in, oxygen mixes with your blood. When you breathe out, your blood lets out carbon dioxide.

Giving Life

Blood feeds your body. When you eat, it carries the food's **nutrients** to your cells and **organs**. It also carries a gas called oxygen to these parts.

Blood **protects** your body, too. It removes waste, such as the gas carbon dioxide. It helps fight **germs**. And, it helps your brain understand what your body needs.

When you eat an orange, your blood carries vitamin C to where your body needs it.

Your blood is made up of three types of cells. These are red blood cells, white blood cells, and platelets.

Each type of cell has a different job. Red blood cells carry oxygen and carbon dioxide. White blood cells fight **germs** and sickness. Platelets help you stop bleeding if you have a cut.

All of these cells move in a watery liquid called plasma. Plasma contains waste products and important **nutrients**.

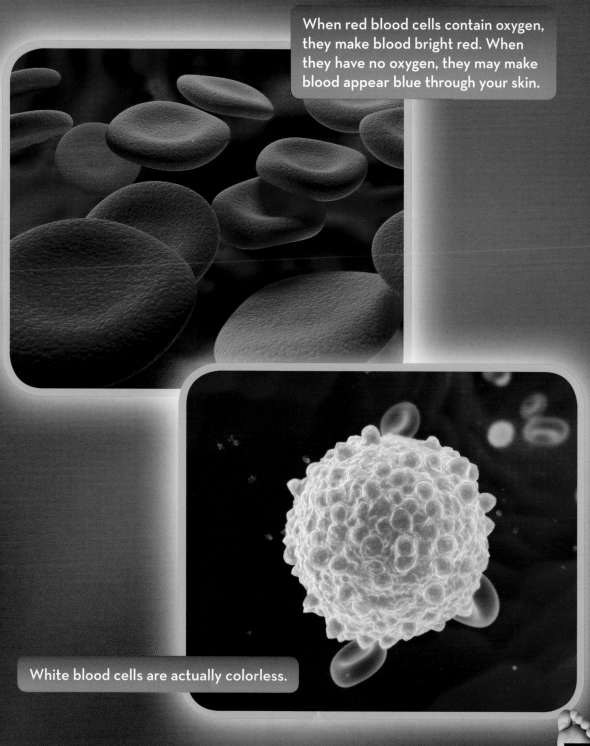

When red blood cells contain oxygen, they make blood bright red. When they have no oxygen, they may make blood appear blue through your skin.

White blood cells are actually colorless.

Your body has billions of platelets. They are very tiny.

Protecting and Healing

When you get a cut, your blood helps **protect** and heal you. At first, blood flows out. Then, platelets stick to each other and the skin to slow blood flow.

Soon, platelets let out **chemicals** that help make sticky fibers. Red blood cells and platelets get caught in the fibers. These form a solid plug called a clot. Later, the clot hardens into a scab.

Scabs protect your skin while it heals underneath.

From the Heart

Everyone has a heart. Your heart is a **muscular organ**. It is slightly bigger than your fist. It pumps blood through your body.

Your heart is just left of the center of your chest. Your spine, ribs, and breastbone **protect** it. Blood vessels connect your heart to every body part.

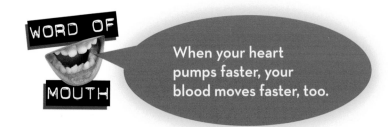

WORD OF MOUTH

When your heart pumps faster, your blood moves faster, too.

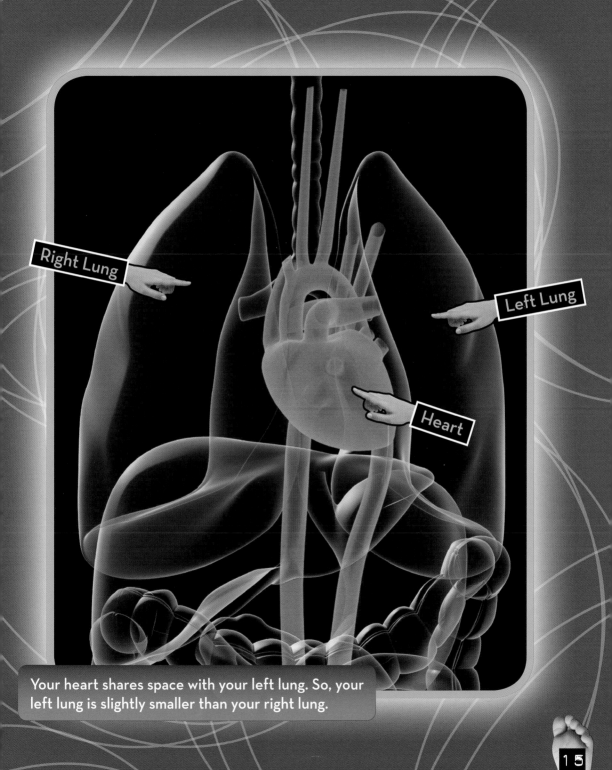

Right Lung

Left Lung

Heart

Your heart shares space with your left lung. So, your left lung is slightly smaller than your right lung.

Movable flaps called valves help move blood through the heart. They act as doors. When valves close, they make a noise. This is your heartbeat.

The heart has four main parts. The right atrium and the left atrium are at the top. At the bottom are the right ventricle and the left ventricle.

Blood is always entering and exiting your heart. It flows into your right atrium from your body. Then, it passes into your right ventricle. From there, it is pumped into your lungs.

In the lungs, blood lets out carbon dioxide and picks up oxygen. Then, it enters your left atrium. It passes into your left ventricle. From there, it is pumped through your body.

YOUR HEART

Right Atrium

Left Atrium

Right Ventricle

Left Ventricle

A Long Journey

Blood vessels connect your heart to your body parts. They are like a system of pipes through your body. Types of blood vessels include arteries, capillaries, and veins.

Arteries carry blood away from the heart. When your heart pumps, blood is pushed out in fast, hard bursts. Arteries have thicker walls than other blood vessels. That way, they can handle fast-moving blood!

YOUR BLOOD VESSELS

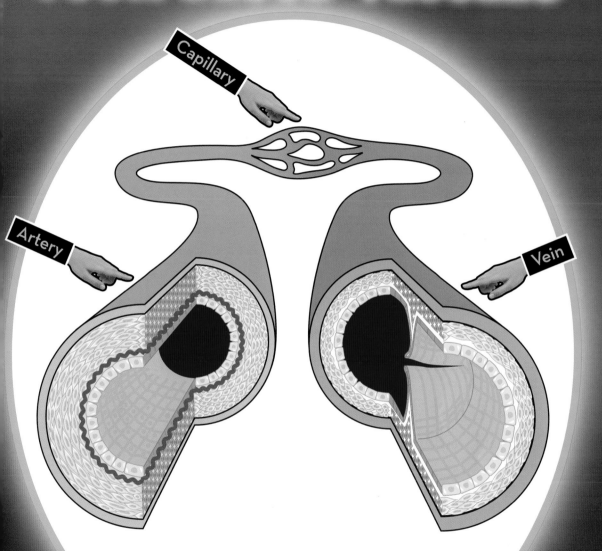

As blood travels around the body, the arteries become smaller and smaller. From these small vessels, blood enters your capillaries.

In capillaries, blood passes oxygen and **nutrients** into cells. It also collects waste and carbon dioxide.

From the capillaries, blood enters your veins. Veins carry blood back to the heart. Blood moves through them with less force. So, veins have thinner walls than arteries.

WORD OF

MOUTH

Your body has organs that help clean your blood. Your spleen, liver, and kidneys remove waste from your blood.

Capillary walls are very thin. Nutrients and waste pass through easily. Ten capillaries together are thinner than one human hair!

Brain Food

What's your type?

Did you know that people have different kinds of blood? The main types are A, B, AB, or O. A person's type depends on **chemicals** in the blood.

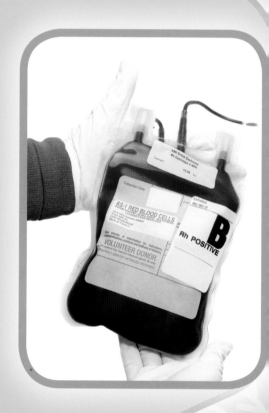

When did doctors first start fixing hearts?

Dr. Daniel Hale Williams performed the first successful open heart operation in Chicago in 1893.

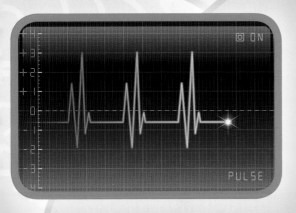

How does your heart know how fast to beat?

There is a special part of your heart called the pacemaker. It sets your heart's rate. If this part stops working, doctors can help. They can replace it with a man-made pacemaker.

You can learn a lot about your health from your blood. Nurses use needles to draw blood and test it.

Glug Glug

Eating unhealthy foods or becoming overweight can harm your circulatory system. These can cause high **blood pressure** and block blood vessels.

The circulatory system can have other problems, too. For example, people can have a condition called anemia. Their blood lacks enough red blood cells. This may cause them to feel weak or tired.

Foods high in fat or salt are unhealthy. Fat can block arteries. Salt may cause high blood pressure.

Doctors can help with many circulatory system problems. They have tools to listen to your heart. Doctors also have tools to check inside your veins and arteries.

Heart, blood, and blood vessel problems can become serious. However, doctors are often able to fix or replace parts that don't work.

WORD OF MOUTH

Some people get man-made hearts. These machines pump blood. They are made to replace natural hearts.

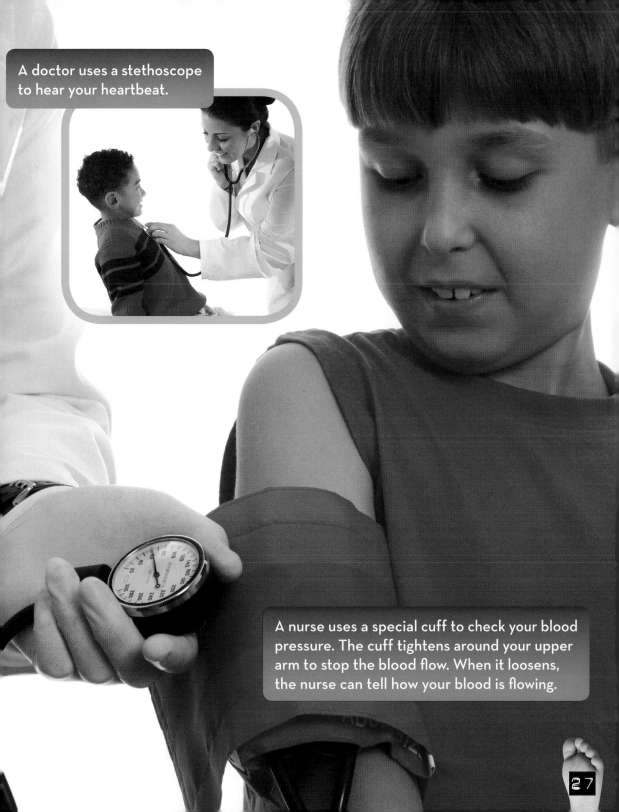

A doctor uses a stethoscope to hear your heartbeat.

A nurse uses a special cuff to check your blood pressure. The cuff tightens around your upper arm to stop the blood flow. When it loosens, the nurse can tell how your blood is flowing.

Your heart pumps about 2.4 ounces (70 ml) of blood into the arteries with each beat. It does this 60 to 100 times each minute!

WORD OF MOUTH

An Important System

Think of how much happens with each heartbeat! Your circulatory system runs on its own. Still, you can **protect** it by learning more about it. Then, you can make good choices to keep your body healthy.

Blood banks collect and store all blood types. They give hospitals blood to match each patient's blood type.

HEALTHY BODY FILES

WORK IT OUT

✔ Being active for one hour each day gets your heart pumping fast. This keeps your heart strong.

✔ Running, walking, and swimming are just a few ways to strengthen your circulatory system.

SHINY TEETH

✔ Some scientists believe the germs that cause plaque and gum disease also cause heart disease. Brush and floss your teeth regularly to prevent this.

EAT RIGHT

✔ Eating healthy foods, such as fruits and veggies, keeps arteries clear and blood pressure low.

Important Words

blood pressure (BLUHD PREH-shuhr) the force your blood puts against your blood vessels as your heart pumps.

chemical (KEH-mih-kuhl) a substance that can cause reactions and changes.

germs (JUHRMS) harmful organisms that can make people sick.

muscular (MUHS-kyuh-luhr) having strong, well-developed muscles. Muscles are body tissues, or layers of cells, that help the body move.

nutrient (NOO-tree-uhnt) something found in food that living beings take in for growth and development.

organ a body part that does a special job. The heart and the lungs are organs.

process a natural order of actions.

protect (pruh-TEHKT) to guard against harm or danger.

Web Sites

To learn more about the circulatory system, visit ABDO Publishing Company online. Web sites about the circulatory system are featured on our Book Links page. These links are routinely monitored and updated to provide the most current information available.

www.abdopublishing.com

Index

arteries **7, 18, 19, 20, 25, 26, 28, 30**

blood **4, 6, 8, 9, 10, 11, 12, 14, 16, 18, 19, 20, 22, 24, 25, 26, 27, 28, 29, 30**

brain **6, 8**

capillaries **18, 19, 20, 21**

carbon dioxide **8, 10, 16, 20**

health **8, 10, 12, 13, 23, 24, 25, 26, 27, 28, 30**

heart **6, 7, 14, 15, 16, 17, 18, 20, 23, 26, 27, 28, 30**

kidneys **20**

liver **20**

lungs **7, 15, 16**

nutrients **8, 9, 10, 20, 21**

oxygen **8, 10, 11, 16, 20**

pacemaker **23**

plasma **10**

platelets **10, 12**

red blood cells **10, 11, 12, 24**

spleen **20**

veins **7, 18, 19, 20, 26**

waste **8, 10, 20, 21**

white blood cells **10, 11**

Williams, Daniel Hale **23**